THE STORY OF OUR BIBLE

Rhona Pipe

Copyright © 1997 Angus Hudson Ltd/
Tim Dowley & Peter Wyart trading as
Three's Company

First UK edition published in 1997 by
National Bible Society of Scotland

ISBN 0901518220

Designed by Peter Wyart, Three's Company
Illustrations by Peter Dennis
Charts by Jeremy Gower
Co-edition organised and produced by
Angus Hudson Ltd,
Concorde House,
Grenville Place,
Mill Hill,
London NW7 3SA

Printed in Hong Kong

This book was created with the kind assistance of the National Bible Society of Scotland and in conjunction with their innovative Bibleworld exhibition.

Contents

Who wrote the Bible?

Moses

David

Isaiah

Amos

Nehemiah

Moses' parents were slaves in Egypt. He was rescued from death by Pharoah's daughter, and grew up as her son – a prince of Egypt. Later he led the slaves to freedom. He wrote parts of the **first five books** of the Bible.

David was the shepherd boy who knocked out a giant with a stone from his sling. He grew up to be a mighty warrior and his country's best-ever king. He was a poet and a musician and wrote many of the **psalms.**

Isaiah, the friend and adviser of kings, was God's spokesperson (a prophet) in Jerusalem about 740 years before Jesus was born. In the Bible book, **Isaiah**, we can read Isaiah's messages from God to the world.

Amos was a farmer who hated the cheating, bullying, greed and sham worship of God that he saw in the market towns of Israel. So he stood up at Bethel and spoke out for God. Told to clear off, he wrote down his message in the book of **Amos.**

Nehemiah, a VIP in the palace of the Persian Emperor, was given leave of absence to organize the rebuilding of Jerusalem. He faced jeers, lies and threats of sabotage and murder. The book of **Nehemiah** has extracts from Nehemiah's diary.

Oral tradition

The first stories in the Bible go back long before writing was invented. They were passed on in the same way that children's playground songs are passed on – by constant repetition. Passing stories on in this way is often called oral, or spoken, tradition. Round the camp-fires in the evenings, at worship, at work or at war, the people sang the songs and told the stories they had learnt as children. Because the stories were about God, they were treated with great respect. Every word was important, and had to be recited correctly.

In New Testament times, too, many hundreds of years later, stories about Jesus were at first passed on by word of mouth. The four Gospels – Matthew, Mark, Luke and John – were based on eye-witness accounts of Jesus' life.

BIBLE FACTS
Contents: Sixty-six books (Catholic Bible 72 books)
Authors: Many – at least thirty
Author-in-chief: God
Time span: 2,000 years
Subjects: Include history, biography, poetry and letters.
Importance: Tells the truth about God and this world.

Mark

When Mark (full name, John Mark) was young, Jesus' friends met in an upper room in his mother's house in Jerusalem. Later he was an assistant to both Peter and Paul. After Peter was killed in Rome, Mark wrote down Peter's teaching in what we know as **Mark's Gospel.**

John

John was a fisherman who became one of Jesus' closest friends. As well as **John's Gospel** the New Testament has three letters by John, and the book of **Revelation**, which John wrote when he was a prisoner on the island of Patmos.

Paul and company

Luke, Paul's doctor, wrote **Luke's Gospel**, and also **Acts** – the story of the first Christians. In the New Testament there are twenty-one personal letters, written to help new Christians. Their authors include Paul, and Jesus' brother James, and Jesus' friend Peter.

How the Bible was written

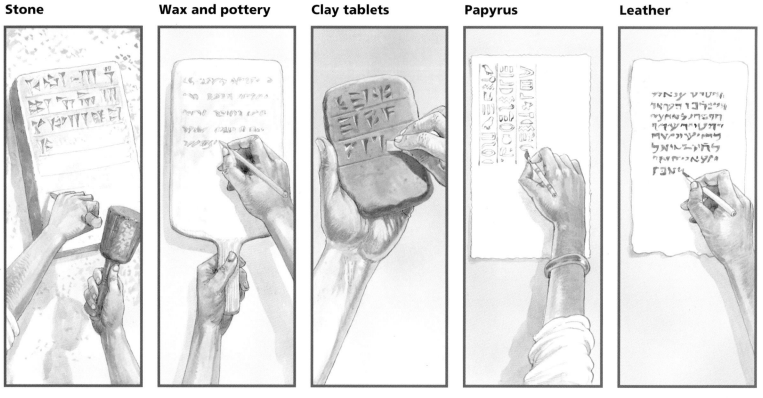

Stone

Wax and pottery

Clay tablets

Papyrus

Leather

The first permanent writing surface was stone. On cave walls in France there are stone-age paintings that are 35,000 years old. In the Bible, the first reference to writing is to the Ten Commandments, which were written on stone. The first pen was a chisel.

Writing boards were made from pieces of wood or ivory covered with wax. Two boards were sometimes hinged together. Any pointed stick made a pen. Broken pottery came in handy for memos, bills and even shopping lists. Ink was soot mixed with oil or gum.

In ancient Babylonia clay was shaped into thin, flat, rectangular bricks. Words were pressed into the soft clay with a wedge-shaped stylus, and then the clay was baked in the sun. Archaeologists have found whole libraries of these clay tablets.

Before the pyramids were built, ancient Egyptians had learnt to make papyrus paper from the pith of Nile reeds. Papyrus was expensive but could be reused by washing, or by scraping. Egyptian pens were brushes made from reeds.

In Israel the skins of sheep and goats were dried, scraped and cleaned to make a smooth material called parchment. (The Hebrew word for book means 'scrape'.) Pens were reeds with one end cut in a slight slope and then split.

Writing

The first writing was made up of simple pictures – one picture for each word. Writing like this, with over 800 pictures, has been found in Babylonia (modern Iraq) and is over 5,000 years old.

Egyptians made up their own small pictures to represent words or parts of words and painted them on walls or papyrus sheets.

Babylonian people did not have papyrus, and it was not easy to draw on clay. Their pictures became simpler until words were shapes pressed into the clay with wedge-shaped sticks. 'Cuneiform' means 'wedge-shaped'.

The alphabet

In Canaan about 1500 BC someone had the clever idea of making up a symbol – a letter – for each sound in the language. This came to about 25 letters. Now there was no need to learn hundreds of shapes for hundreds of words. Any word could be written down just by listening to its sounds and choosing the matching letters. This simple idea quickly spread.

PAPYRUS

Papyrus plants are large reeds, between three and six metres high. They grew abundantly by the River Nile, and were sometimes found along the banks of the Jordan River in Israel.

HOW TO MAKE PAPYRUS

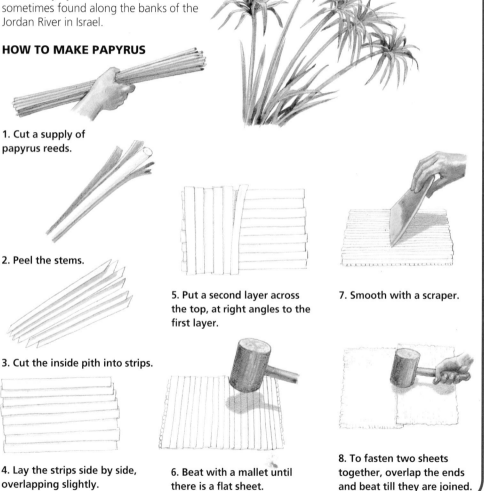

1. **Cut a supply of papyrus reeds.**

2. **Peel the stems.**

3. **Cut the inside pith into strips.**

4. **Lay the strips side by side, overlapping slightly.**

5. **Put a second layer across the top, at right angles to the first layer.**

6. **Beat with a mallet until there is a flat sheet.**

7. **Smooth with a scraper.**

8. **To fasten two sheets together, overlap the ends and beat till they are joined.**

The languages of the Bible

Hebrew Scribe

In Bible times, very few people could read and write. If they needed to send a letter, or to have a letter read to them, they went to a scribe. The scribe was an important person in a town: he sat near the town gate, making legal documents and writing letters.

Hebrew Alphabet

אבגדהוזחטיכלמנסעפצקרשת

Hebrew

The Old Testament tells the story of the Israelite people. Their language was Hebrew, and therefore most of the Old Testament is written in Hebrew. The Hebrew alphabet has twenty-two consonants, but no vowels (vowel sounds were added by the reader). Hebrew is read from right to left so the first page of the Hebrew Bible is our last page.

Aramaic

Aramaic was spoken by the Persians, who were the super-power in the world for two hundred years from about 550 BC. Aramaic became the language used by traders world-wide. In the Old Testament, parts of Daniel, Ezra and Jeremiah are in Aramaic.

By New Testament times Aramaic was the everyday language of the Jews, while Hebrew remained the language for prayer and worship. Educated people still understood Hebrew, but when the Hebrew Bible was read aloud in synagogue services, a translator often gave the meaning.

Greek

In 331 BC the Greek general Alexander the Great conquered Persia and ruled the world. Then Greek became the language that most people understood. When the followers of Jesus wrote the New Testament, they wanted the whole world to know the good news. So they wrote in Greek, giving us a Greek translation of the Aramaic spoken by Jesus. A few times they kept the Aramaic original. *Abba* is an Aramaic word meaning 'Dad'.

When Jesus spoke to a dead girl, he said, *'Talitha, koum'* – these were his actual Aramaic words (look up Mark 5:41). The Gospel writers gave us the Greek translation, which in English is, 'Little girl, I tell you to stand up.'

There are twenty-four letters in the Greek alphabet, which was the first alphabet to include letters for vowels. Sentences were written from left to right.

Greek Alphabet

The first Christian writings

Possibly the earliest part of the New Testament so far discovered is a papyrus fragment (only six cm by nine cm) containing a few lines from John's Gospel (John 18:31-33, 37-38). It is written in Greek and dates from about AD 130, and is sometimes called the John Rylands Fragment.

The scroll

When the Bible was written, books with pages had not been invented. Instead, people wrote on 'scrolls'. These were made from sheets of papyrus or parchment (or even thin copper) that had been sewn or glued together to form a long strip, up to thirty feet long and twelve inches wide. Each end was wound round a wooden rod and while reading the reader unrolled the scroll with one hand and rolled it up with the other. When not in use, scrolls were wrapped in cloths and stored in tall jars.

Dead Sea Scrolls

In 1947 a shepherd at Qumran, by the Dead Sea, noticed a hole in the cliff. He went to explore and found some stone jars. Inside the jars were rolls of parchment covered with old Hebrew writing. Later, many more scrolls were found in nearby caves.

They turned out to be the library of a Jewish religious sect, and they include parts of every book in the Bible except Esther. Carbon dating has shown that they were written between 200 BC and AD 70. The scroll of Isaiah is 1000 years older than our next oldest copy of Isaiah, yet the two texts are almost identical.

The book

Codex Sinaiticus in book form.

A page from the Codex Sinaiticus.

Scrolls were cumbersome to carry, and it was time-consuming to find a short Bible passage on a long scroll. Second century Christians were collecting the books of the New Testament and were probably the first people to do away with the scroll. Instead, they hit on the idea of putting together several sheets of papyrus or parchment, folding them in half, sewing along the fold, and then adding more folded sheets. This forerunner of our 'book' was sometimes also given a harder cover. It was called a *codex* (plural *codices*).

Our earliest complete copy of the New Testament was written not long after AD 300. It is called *Codex Sinaiticus* because it was found in a monastery at the foot of Mount Sinai.

Bible fact

By AD 100 all our New Testament books had been written. They were slowly collected together to form a 'canon' or 'measuring rod' of the Christian faith.

How did the Bible come down to us?

Jewish Scribes

Monks

When new copies of Old Testament scrolls were needed, every word had to be written out by hand. The scribes were the men who had the task of keeping safe, copying out and explaining the teaching of the Old Testament.

To make sure that each scribe understood the importance of his work, and to stop him making mistakes, careful rules were followed. For example:

• Each day he had to start his work with a prayer.

• The name of God had to be left blank, to be filled in later by a different scribe, using a 'purer' ink.

• At the end of a section of a book, the scribe counted the lines, the words, and the letters and checked them with his copy. He also found and checked the middle word of each section.

Sometimes mistakes were made. But it has been computed that mistakes averaged out at only one mistake in every 1,580 letters!

The word 'monk' comes from a Greek word meaning 'someone who lives alone'. The first Christian monk was Antony, who lived by himself in the desert from about AD 270-290. Others followed his example. More often men (and, separately, women) lived in groups in monasteries, spending their days in prayer, Bible study and useful work such as farming or nursing.

During the Dark Ages after the fall of the Roman Empire, it was the monks who protected and passed on the Bible. When a Bible book was worn out, they spent months and years making a fresh copy. Often they worked in a *scriptorium* or writing room, each monk writing in silence at his desk. Because of the danger of fire, the room had no heat and no lighting. The work was tiring. There was a saying , 'Two fingers hold the pen, but the whole body toils.'

Jerome

Jerome was born in northern Italy in about AD 384. He was baptized into the Christian church when he was a student in Rome. He later became a monk.

The Vulgate

By AD 380 most Christians in the West spoke Latin and it was hard for them to understand the Greek New Testament. Many Latin translations had been made, but they were neither well-written nor accurate. Jerome was the cleverest man then living in the West, so the Pope asked him to write a new Latin translation of the Gospels and Psalms. Over the next twenty-two years Jerome worked from the original Hebrew and Greek manuscripts to produce a Latin translation of the entire Bible. His Bible slowly increased in popularity. From the eighth century until 1609 it was the only Bible used by the Roman Catholic church. It was known as *The Vulgate* which means, 'Common Version'.

Precious books

Hand-made books

A book from Iona

Books were made of very fine calfskin (vellum) or the skin of a sheep or goat (parchment). After a monk had finished copying out the Latin words in a beautiful, elegant script, his work was checked. The pages were then decorated in brilliant, glowing colours, and the completed book was bound.

The monks made their own water paints, and also used real gold and silver to 'illuminate' their work. They added borders to the pages, and enlarged and decorated the first letter of a book, chapter or paragraph. They created intricate, interlocking designs of curves, spirals, scrolls, shields and little, detailed paintings of animals and birds.

Irish monks travel
In the fifth and sixth centuries Irish monks travelled to Scotland and northern England, bringing with them the ability to create beautiful and imaginative Celtic designs. Superbly decorated books were produced in remote monasteries on bleak cliffs and islands. A monk might spend his whole life working on one book. It was his way of showing his love for God.

The Book of Kells
In the Celtic *Book of Kells* a small design, only 1.61 sq. cm in size (1/4 sq. in.) is made up of 158 tiny 'interlaced' shapes. This illuminated book of the Gospels in Latin is perhaps the greatest masterpiece of Celtic and Anglo-Saxon art. It was begun in the seventh century in the monastery at Iona, off the west of Scotland. After a Viking raid it was taken for safe-keeping to Kells in Ireland, where it was completed. It consists of 339 leaves, 33 x 25 cms (13 x 10ins) in size. Every page is richly decorated.

Lindisfarne Gospels

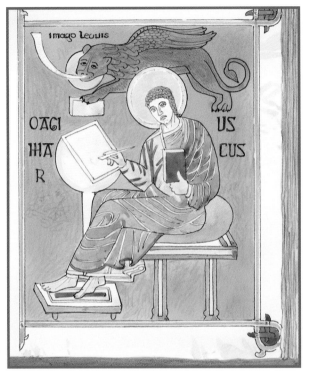

Lindisfarne is a small island off the coast of Northumbria, England, where, in AD 635, monks from Iona established a 'daughter' monastery. The Gospels were copied out and illuminated about AD 700.

Golden Gospels
A series of illuminated manuscripts of the Gospels created in the eighth century in France under the guidance of Alcuin from York in England. The lettering was mainly in gold, and the decoration in silver and gold, all on purple-stained vellum.

Bible in chains
Most Bibles were much less ornate than the *Book of Kells*. and the *Golden Gospels*. But even the simplest books took years to complete. When a Bible was finished, it was put on display in a monastery chapel or cathedral. It was very valuable, and was chained to the reading desk so that no one could steal it.

Early translations of the Bible

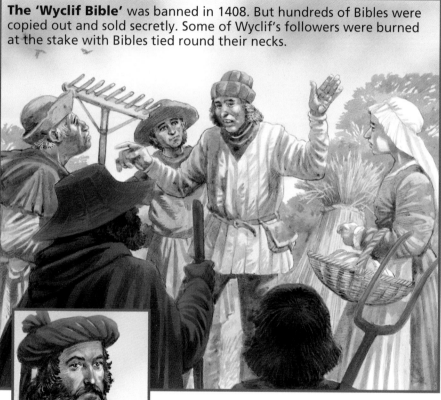

The 'Wyclif Bible' was banned in 1408. But hundreds of Bibles were copied out and sold secretly. Some of Wyclif's followers were burned at the stake with Bibles tied round their necks.

John Wyclif lived from about 1329-1384. He taught at Oxford University until he was thrown out for attacking corruption in the church. Wyclif longed for the Bible to be translated into English so that ordinary people could understand its true teaching. He proposed, and may have partly supervised, the first English translation.

•**Northern Europe** About AD 350 Bishop Ulfilas translated the Bible into the language of the Goths. This Germanic language had never before been written down.

•**Eastern Europe** In the ninth century, two brothers, Cyril and Methodius, who were missionaries among the Slavs, translated the Bible into Old Slavonic. The alphabet they invented was a forerunner of the Cyrillic alphabet, still used today in south-eastern Europe and Russia.

•**France** About 1175, Peter Waldo, a wealthy merchant living in Lyons, became a Christian and gave away all his possessions. His followers (called Waldensians) translated the Bible into Provençal and probably also into Italian, German, Piedmontese (northern Italian) and Catalan (spoken in north-east Spain).

•**England** The first translation into Anglo-Saxon was a version of the Psalms made about AD 700 by Bishop Aldhelm. A translation of the complete Bible into English was not finished until 1384. It was written by followers of Wyclif.

John Hus

In Prague, the capital of Bohemia (now the Czech Republic), the preacher John Hus, influenced by the teaching of Wyclif, began to speak out against the greed, immorality and ambition of priests. As a result, in 1415 he was burnt at the stake. His followers began to translate the Bible into Czech, and the Czech New Testament came out in 1475.

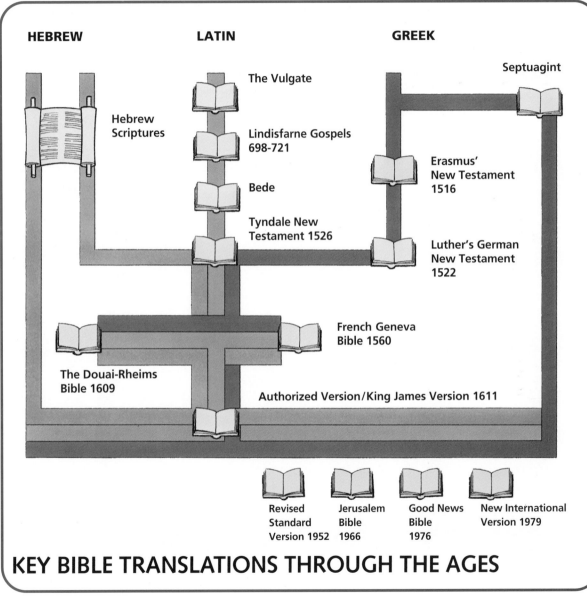

HEBREW

LATIN

GREEK

Septuagint

The Vulgate

Hebrew Scriptures

Lindisfarne Gospels 698-721

Erasmus' New Testament 1516

Bede

Tyndale New Testament 1526

Luther's German New Testament 1522

French Geneva Bible 1560

The Douai-Rheims Bible 1609

Authorized Version/King James Version 1611

Revised Standard Version 1952

Jerusalem Bible 1966

Good News Bible 1976

New International Version 1979

KEY BIBLE TRANSLATIONS THROUGH THE AGES

Printing . . . no more copying!

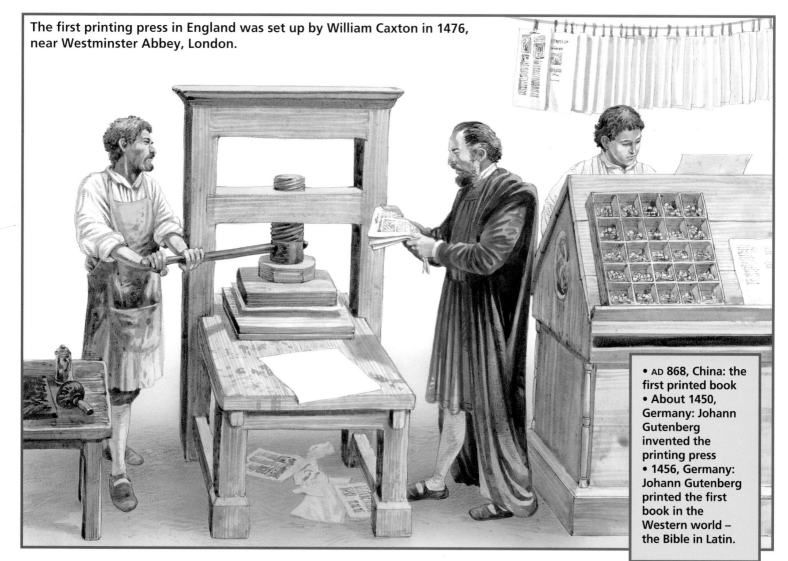

The first printing press in England was set up by William Caxton in 1476, near Westminster Abbey, London.

- AD **868, China: the first printed book**
- **About 1450, Germany: Johann Gutenberg invented the printing press**
- **1456, Germany: Johann Gutenberg printed the first book in the Western world – the Bible in Latin.**

1861 National Bible Society of Scotland (union of Glasgow and Edinburgh)

1805 Glasgow

1816 Norway

1809 Edinburgh

1815 Sweden

1804 **1814** Denmark

1807 Canada

1813 Russia

1806 Ireland

1814 Netherlands

1804 British and Foreign Bible Society

1816 America

1837 New Zealand

1817 Australia

Bible Societies around the World

United Bible Societies

In 1946 the United Bible Societies was formed to co-ordinate the work of the national Societies and give help and advice on Bible translation.

WYCLIFFE BIBLE TRANSLATORS

'If your God is so smart, why doesn't he learn my language?' **William Cameron Townsend** was selling Spanish Bibles to Cakchiquel Indians in Guatemala when he was asked that question. He immediately started to learn Cakchiquel so that he could translate the N Testament and show t Indian that God did care. took him fifteen years. In

1934 he started a training school to teach young missionaries how to live with a tribe, learn and write down their language, translate the Scriptures, and then teach the people to read them. This became the Wycliffe Bible Translators. Today it is the largest missionary n the world, with 00 missionaries .

TRANSLATION FACTS

• **Total number of languages recorded in the world: over 6,500**

Of these:
• **355 have a complete Bible**
• **880 have a New Testament only**
• **2,167 have at least 1 portion of the Bible (These figures were for the end of 1996.)**
• **In 1997 4,333 languages were without even one book of the Bible.**

Modern Technology

Before computer technology it took thirty years from start to finish to translate, check and print a new version of the Bible. Today, translators have portable computers, so that their work does not have to be re-keyed. This, together with computer page-layout, the spell-checker, computerized typesetting and advanced printing techniques, means that the work can be completed in ten years or less and at a much reduced cost.

Words of Hope . . .

David Livingstone

David Livingstone travelled into Africa through jungles and along rivers where no white man had ever been before. He faced terrifying dangers, led on by his longing to show Jesus to the Africans, and to free them from the 'open sore' of the slave trade. In 1886, speaking to students in Glasgow, he said, 'Would you like me to tell you what supported me through all the years of exile? . . . It was this: "Lo, I am with you alway, even unto the end of the world." On these words (of Jesus) I staked everything, and they never failed.'

Kriss Akabusi

When Kriss Akabusi went to Nigeria in 1991 he was greeted by a 21-gun salute. When his father dies, he will be the chief of six villages. But he spent his childhood shunted around children's homes in England. It was in the army that his brilliance as a runner was discovered. In 1986 Kriss went to Edinburgh for the Commonwealth Games. In his hotel room there was a copy of the *Good News Bible* – the New Testament in plain English. He started to read and found himself gripped by the character of Jesus. He says, 'I had never realized that Jesus had walked on earth and said so many amazing things.' He started to investigate whether Jesus had been a historical figure or had been invented by the Bible writers. He found out Jesus had really existed. The following year he went to bed praying, 'Jesus, if you're really who you say you are, let me know.' That night he had a dream in which he heard Jesus saying, 'Come to me all you who are weary and heavy laden and I will give you rest . . . ' These Bible words in his dream clinched everything, and he knew he was loved by God.

Mutiny on The Bounty

On April 28th, 1789, sailors on *The Bounty*, a British ship, rebelled against their captain. Setting him adrift on the Pacific Ocean they sailed to the island of Tahiti. Nine set sail again with twelve native women. Arriving at the lovely deserted island of Pitcairn, they burned *The Bounty* and settled down to a life of bliss.

It turned out to be a drunken, murderous hell. When only two pitiful sailors were left, with the women and eighteen children, one sailor found an old Bible. He started to read it aloud.

After eighteen years a ship arrived at the island. The captain later reported that he had never met any people so good and loving, so peaceful and happy as the group who came to welcome him.

Irina Ratushinskaya

Irina Ratushinskaya, the Russian poet, grew up in Communist Russia. When she was a child, she often prayed to God. She was sure he was real and that he loved her, though she had never seen a Bible. Later, she was given an old Bible, written in Old Slavonic, an ancient, complicated language which no one spoke any longer. She spent six weeks learning the language, and then began to read. Everything fitted into place as she read about Jesus.

In Russia it was dangerous to be a believer and Irina spent years in prison. But she would not give up her faith. She is now living in England.

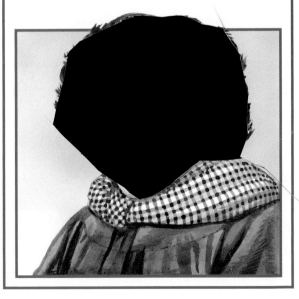

Index